SOUL TRASH, SPACE GARBAGE

POEMS

Michelle Awad

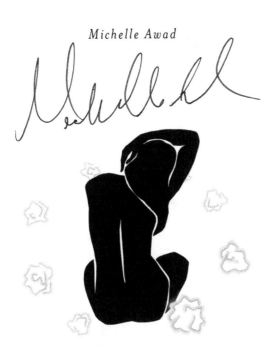

NEW ORLEANS

2021

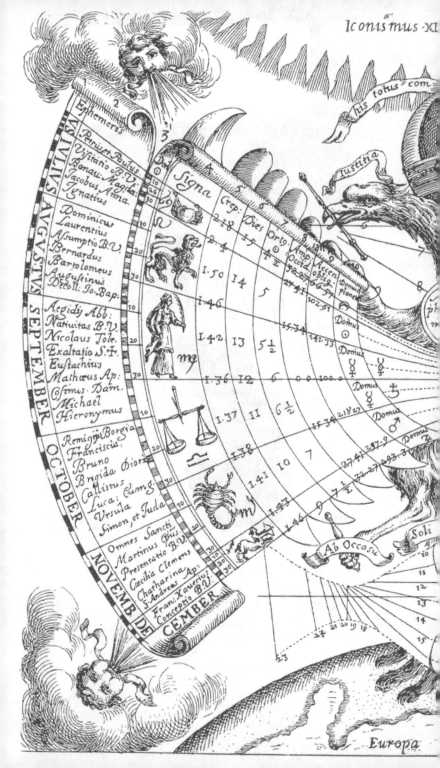

SOUL TRASH,

SPACE GARBAGE

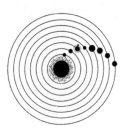

PAPERBACK EDITION - DECEMBER 2021

Book cover and interior design by R. Clift / @r.cliftpoetry

ISBN 978-0-578-93531-7

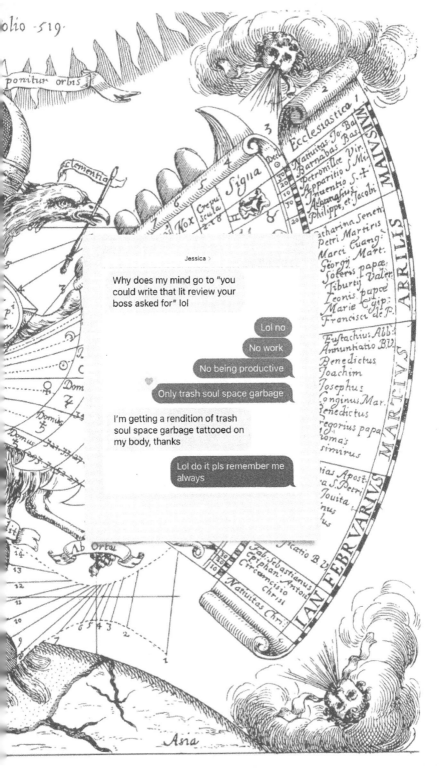

Jessica ›

Why does my mind go to "you could write that lit review your boss asked for" lol

Lol no

No work

No being productive

Only trash soul space garbage

I'm getting a rendition of trash soul space garbage tattooed on my body, thanks

Lol do it pls remember me always

TO THE PEOPLE WHO TOOK WHAT WAS JUST THE STARDUST
OF A LITTLE GIRL, AND TURNED HER INTO A UNIVERSE OF
A WOMAN

i have inside of me a few stars that look suspiciously like angels, i hold a few
galaxies that make me believe in god.
you
are all of them.
they are all of
you.

HONORABLE MENTIONS

Nicole Ting / @elocinting
e. e. cummings
Tom Robbins
Tawny Platis / @tawnyplatis
Sei Shonagon
Zane Frederick / @zanefrederickwrites
Kim Addonizio / @kimaddonizio
Tony Hoagland
Victoria Chang
Amy Kay / @amykaypoetry
Lemony Snicket
Tabitha Sears
And a special thanks to Space.com, TechExplorist.com, and TechTimes.com
for some excellent article headlines turned poem titles

TABLE OF CONTENTS

WHITE DWARF

*Small stars, similar in size to the Sun, undergo a relatively peaceful and beautiful death in which they pass through a planetary nebula phase to become what's called a **white dwarf**. The star corpse eventually cools down and simply stops glowing.*

there was candlelight
and loud music,
and your shirt tucked in
and me wanting to un-tuck it,
(I'm getting ahead of myself
wait let me start again) in the
beginning, there was
candlelight, and it bounced off
your face like the moon off
the city, and there was swimming,
or just the feeling of swimming,
holding my breath, and buoyancy,
and air cold, and lips wet, and
you ask me what I like to drink,
and I say *I-don't-know, something-with
gin-in-it,* and suddenly the bar
was flooded
with the hope of something
built to withstand anything.

There was telling your friends and meeting
my family. There was coming home too
late. There was leaving too early. There was
kissing you and kissing you and kissing
you and kissing you and
falling asleep accidentally.

We broke bread, we mended
fences, we made little promises we
weren't sure
we could keep. In the end,

there was
firelight and Western Honey Pepper
Whiskey, and the sound of ice clinking.
There was a voice off in the distance, but it wasn't
you, and it wasn't me; it sounded like *sorry,* and *stay
here,* and

please.

ANAGRAMS FOR EDEN

roots buried. a transplant. magnolia trees. a trombone singing.
dark rum. and bubblegum. you find my stretch marks. and write
your name in between them. we speak in tongues. holy water.
father's daughter. outside, it's storming. the angels bowl. god
takes up photography. he finds us beautiful. the devil, too. our
symmetry. they both concede. the things we don't know only
hurt us a little. only make us. feel lonely. I take a bite of the apple
in your throat. you blame me for everything I tell you I
need.

FATHERHOOD AND CREATIONISM ARE THE SAME STORY

I burst forth,
slimy,
sticky,
slippery,
red,
I never stopped
being red, actually,
crying,
always crying,
maybe that's why
I try not to
lately,
they gave me
to my mother,
and she laughed,
what the hell
am I gonna
do with you,
my father
was in the room,
or maybe he wasn't,
probably he wasn't,
the second thing
I knew
after the warmth of
the womb
was that the world
was cold, too. My father,

the Great Collector,
of bar stools, and gas
station receipts, of
more women's children
than he knew
what to do with; I thank
whatever God
there is
for my mother,
lying there,
slimy,
sticky,
slippery,
red, unafraid
to be red, with me,

they gave me
to her, this tiny,
wrinkled thing, and she
laughed,
what the hell
am I gonna
do with you,
she said, and she never got an answer
any more
than he did.

But she stayed anyway.

THE BIG BANG

My twenty-year-old self comes home half-drunk and half-alone, gives herself to anyone who comes across half-worthy. Gives you her reds, her golds, her blues (mostly her blues). Gets weirded out by dudes who want to talk on the phone instead of text, never answers as a way to keep them at arms' length.

My fourteen-year-old self reads vampire fiction like she will live forever. Doodles last names of secret crushes in her notebook then watches them fall for her friends, every time. Is obsessed with serial killers and cities she's never slept in. Thinks all the boys are just leftover gentlemen, never quite as good as the ones who came before them.

My seven-year-old self plays with dinosaur figurines, collects pinecones from the wooded area behind her house, doesn't go home until the streetlights come calling. Already knows that men love alibis and leaving, above most things; thinks there's no way Santa comes down the chimney because he wouldn't make that much effort to see me; learned about the world ending and wondered
if it was pretty.

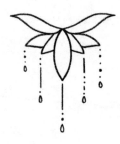

TICKS, CHIGGERS, AND THE THINGS MY
MOTHER TAUGHT ME

If you pee in your pants, you'll drown Barney.

You have to brush your teeth every day, or they'll all
fall out, and then you won't have any.

They usually won't pull you over if you're
only going 5 miles over the speed limit.

All I know is, if you have the option
to either laugh or to cry, then laugh, dammit. No matter
how dark it is, make a joke about it. I paid a lot of money
for that smile, and I want to see it.

You got your sense of humor from your Grandfather.

If a man ever makes you feel like you're not
good enough, leave. If he forgets your anniversary, leave.
If he lies to you, leave. After I had you, your father told me
he wasn't attracted to me anymore, but he was the one to

leave, and it should have been
me.

Life is too short to feel like you're
missing something.

Expiration dates are just
recommendations.

Goodbyes are just I'm sorrys.

8-YEAR-OLD BRAZILIAN GIRL CALLED "WORLD'S YOUNGEST ASTRONOMER"

and I hope
that she studies
herself,

first and foremost,
fistful
of stardust, sparkling
in the empty—space glitter
across a black canvas, a void she
can work with. she
is all the colors
at once, and she is
none of them at all; they dangle
cutouts of her above babies' beds
so that they might grow up
in her image; and I hope
she aims her telescope
at her face
most nights, takes note of her
constellations, the bridge of her
nose, her light refracting from
flimsy lens, breaking
the sound barrier when she laughs,
asteroids for tears, brain squishy
and grey, something we don't
understand, an alien life form,
initial contact; when she says,
take me to your leader,

we don't move a muscle.

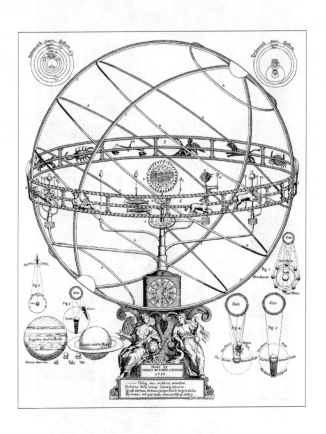

WHEN THE POEM IS A MAGIC LAMP,
YOU RUB IT AND SAY
after Kim Addonizio

Give me homemade biscuits at 9am, fresh out of my
grandmother's oven; the strawberry preserves she
keeps jarred in the basement until she runs out,
sweet and sticking to my fingers, crimson; she says there's
sugar in my blood. I want to sit in that old gazebo
they tore down twenty years ago; I want to remember
what prayer feels like.
Give me my grandfather cracking walnuts in a metal
folding chair under the tree; I want him handing them
to me by the pieces. I want tucking your hair behind
your ear before you leave for work in the morning; and
clementine oranges; and calla lilies. I want to never take
another phone call as long as I live; I want this old
VHS player to never stop working.
Give me my mother's voice like a recording in my chest, as a
music box, my uvula as a ballerina, twirling; don't tell her
I said that. Give me powdered sugar and vanilla
iced coffee; give me a sunny, lazy Saturday at Mojo
on Magazine Street. I want nothing but penance and poetry.
Give me your worst days, your fleeting euphoria; I want
to know every song you ever sang. I want to drain
the Mississippi with a silly straw after they said it
couldn't be done.
I want to hear them say I'm the one who's Mighty.

I want to believe it.

HEREDITY

On days like today, the rain against the roof
feels like bullets in my sides, and the air is
too cold for summer, and I can suddenly
remember my grandmother's fingers snapping
green beans on the carport, the smell of bread in
the oven, the way she laughs while she's crying
like her body is
rejecting it.

When my grandfather passed away, she hid in the
bathroom at the VA hospital, and I stood outside the door,
but I did not press my ear to listen.
All I could hear was the sound of
not breathing.

When she came out, her eyes were not red,
her eyes do not grow red with grief,
her eyes are clear like a lighthouse from out at sea,
her eyes are like the ones that
she gave me.

And months later, it was always the little things—
she hears "Blue Christmas" on the radio,
she breaks down,
an appointment card arrives in the mail for
him, she breaks down.
The crying comes just before the laughter bubbles up
from her throat and erupts into the
living room.

We were not built for sadness,
the women in my family.

We were only built
for enduring.

THINGS THAT MAKE ONE'S HEART BEAT FASTER
after Sei Shonagon

The movement of a hand. To pass a police car while speeding.
To receive correspondence out of the blue from a person one
spent their youth loving. To be next in line. To write poetry.
To hear a noise in the dark of the hall at night after watching a
scary movie, to keep still, to squint at shadows, to wait to hear it
again, to scarcely breathe; there is more rush in the in-between
than there is in the happening.

It is morning, and his side of the bed is empty
when it shouldn't be.
A songbird. A scarecrow. A half-remembered dream.
The dog barks for no reason.

The reason can't be seen.

HOW GRIEF FITS

it's like
the way your
hands shrink
when they get
cold, my rings
become
loose, i cannot keep
you wrapped
around my little
finger any longer.
i lose you.

I HAVE A LOT OF BIG FEELINGS,
AND ONE OF THEM IS

anger and one of them is dread and one of them is
longing and one of them is panic and one of them is just
an ache in my chest, I can't explain it with science, but
sometimes the sound of goodbye is like the click of a
switchblade, the thought that you don't want me is the shape
of a noose, I put my head through but you're not on the other
side. I have a lot of big feelings, and one of them is
I still cry at the sight of my own blood, I've been a woman
since I was a child, I moved to a city that knows how to
survive, between the fires and the floods, between this
and the afterlife, you realize, either way, dying is dying.
I have a lot of big feelings, and one of them is failure and
one of them is pride and one of them is wet face and burning
eyes and one of them is a throb in my temple like an ice pick,
I can't explain it with science, but my molecules are trying to
poison me from the inside.

I have a lot of big feelings, and one of them is fear and one of them
is fear and one of them is fear; I have a lot of big feelings
and all of them are the fear of something,
and all of them are deny,
deny, deny.

QUARANTINE: DAY 43—

I have scratched all the
polish from my fingernails.

I undo my manicure with my
teeth, you offer to get me the
clippers, but I say it's okay; just
another thing I think
I don't need.

You stare at your phone
and show me
the six-hundredth
meme, and I smile
weakly, then back to my
computer screen.

For the first time in over a
year, I write poetry I have no
intention
of you ever reading.

I imagine

I feel hungry but cannot
be bothered to eat
the same way
you don't think about
having sex with me.

Numbly.
Absentmindedly.
Honestly.

You still ask for a kiss
when you have done
a good thing.

I thank you for making
lunch again (kiss), I thank
you for bringing me
my phone charger (kiss),
I thank you
because you love me, and
I feel guilty
that it doesn't seem to be
enough lately.

(Kiss)

Stay inside, they
said, it's safer, they
said.

What if we're already
sick?

MY SIXTEEN-YEAR-OLD HEART AS A BEACH DAY

A car backfired outside my window,
or maybe it was a gunshot,
but either way, my heart
stuttered, like being at a concert
where the bass is heavy
but the rhythm makes you
want to move,
like you are made of mud and
simple syrup,
like the moon knows
all the decent things you don't do
but you mean to.

I carried a knife
between my teeth through the
metallic taste of blood,
gouged my eyes out with spoons
so maybe they could see
something other than the look on your face
when you said you were sorry,
(you were always sorry,)
((you were never sorry,))
but your eyes were blue enough
to take me away,
to make me forget that the ocean
never stays for long at my blistered feet,

despite the promises
it makes.

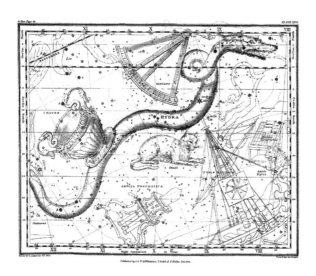

AN EXOPLANET ORBITING THREE
SUNS WAS JUST DETECTED, BUT HOW?

The same way
I told you
what I needed, and you said
it was crazy, how I showed you
I was suffering, and you wouldn't
believe the data; the same way
I gave you those years
of my youth, how I told you
I loved you, how I knew
I couldn't breathe
outside of
your atmosphere,
but you insisted
I could leave
whenever
I wanted to.

IF MY HEART BREAKS AND NO ONE'S AROUND
TO HEAR IT, DOES IT MAKE A SOUND?

contrary to popular belief, it is nothing like glass shattering;
though the shards are the same, made up of sharp edges, a
surface too smooth to forgo the risk of touching.

it is Sunday, and my bed is spider's web silk sticky, sheets spun
around broken body, a cocoon that doesn't end in beauty,
most days, a place to be still in, to be buried;
I make a grave of sleep and it's
somehow always
and never empty.

what they don't tell you

is sometimes heartbreak comes to you like a baby crying
sometimes like a cough you can't shake
sometimes like an elegy you didn't know you were writing.

contrary to popular belief, it is nothing like glass shattering;
it's the silence before impact, it's stepping strategically.

it's the cleaning.

TO THE TUNE OF "SHIMMER" BY FUEL

I don't know what you look like
when I'm not wearing my
glasses: blurry, lying on the couch
after a
long day, undefined at the nose
and mouth and
eyes, too close to my face to make
out anything, like someone you
only know in a dreamscape—
         Intimately.
My perfume is pink now, instead
of blue. My hair is longer. The radio
just doesn't do it for me anymore; I
listen to the same four songs
on repeat and pretend it's not the
soundtrack to
getting over you.

I SPENT FIVE HOURS IN 30TH STREET STATION
AND ALL I GOT WAS THIS LOUSY POEM

too many windows

not enough doors

my feet up on the back of the
seat in front of me

your fingers
trace the seam of my jeans
like I am made
of destinations, like I am
not a home but I am still a
place to sleep

the voice on the intercom
always muffled, always louder
than worth hearing

I switch feet,
the number 12 to New Jersey
leaves

a blue-eyed boy whose
fear of commitment I mistook for
adventure, a jet setter who'd never
seen the sea

the little roundtrip girl that
your love turned into a
weigh station

all your comings and goings

A BEGINNER'S GUIDE
TO BAD MENTAL HEALTH DAYS

sometimes, what i need is
quiet. time to accept all the things that are
weighing on me.

they say that Monday is the worst day of the week,
but have you ever felt that Sunday sunken ship in your
chest cavity, that serotonin dip that sleep won't fix,
that second day of the weekend mourning?

tell me to drink more water.
ask if i want to watch a movie.
say nothing, but sit with me, and let the silence
soak up all the noise in my head, hold me
until it's only a whisper of a breath.

i don't know why i wrote this poem.
i need to give the dog a bath, i need to
fold the laundry. i need to respond to ten different people
about twenty different things, but i just
don't have it in me.

i am sick of only having time for things i don't
enjoy but are simply necessary.
i am tired of finding time but never finding
the energy.

i don't know when Sunday became this monster of a thing;
it makes Monday feel like a reprieve.

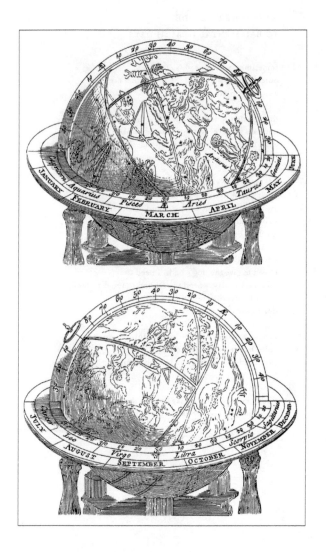

FIRST OLD BINARY STAR CLUSTER DISCOVERED
WITHIN OUR GALAXY

"Both clusters are locked in a gravitational dance that is slowly tearing them apart, leaving smaller clusters and trails of stars in their wake."

I walked barefoot home from Prom. Heels in hand, sparkling under
the breath of streetlights, glistening like morning dew at
midnight.
Somewhere, thrown on upper closet shelves, or stuffed in
under-bed shoeboxes, there is a video of us swaying to music from
the late 2000s; our DNA still in that hotel room; the rhinestones
on that blue dress holding onto your fingerprints in the thrift store
of a city I don't even
live in anymore—

It's funny how people talk about science like it isn't just poetry
that can be proven. Like it isn't your forehead sweat on my bare
shoulder, my laugh in your mouth like an endless echo.
It's hard to have a voice in a vacuum.
We forgot ourselves in nightstand drawers, in dirty cup holders,
in old jewelry boxes where we got inexplicably tangled.
When you spend years tying the knot, it's hard to ever feel
untethered.

I lost morsels of myself like star fragments, a cosmic ricochet,
a celestial shedding: the glint in my eyes, the ring on my finger,
the bright of my smile, the red in my hair like a sunlit penny—
something you don't mind
leaving.

What did you lose, other than me?

THE POEM IS A GIRL MISUNDERSTOOD

The poem
grinds on you at night,
makes shapes with her
body you couldn't read
if you tried, speaks
another language, but
you like it. All you know is
you like it.
The poem takes her tea
with two sugars, her coffee
iced, she takes her time.
They say she must have
been a lawyer in a past life.
The poem lies, the poem
never lies.
She listens to Tony Bennett,
looks at you with wasted
ink irises. The poem
takes out a knife.
From stomach to sternum,
she pours out her insides. It's quiet,
the first time you
see her cry. A sidewalk met
with blood and star dust,
innuendo and rhyme,
and you don't get it, but

you like it. All you know is
you like it.

WEEKEND AT BERNARD MICKEY WRANGLE'S

an homage to Tom Robbins' Still Life with Woodpecker

He asks me, "what's it like
to never want a cigarette?" and I
start laughing, think back to all the
times I've had to explain to a man why I
didn't love him; why I couldn't, in time;
what it was about him that didn't turn my stomach
to an insectarium, my mind to a world map,
my blood to a bottle rocket; why I never felt
compelled to bite his chin, or reach for his
hand, and I say: I have spent so much time
apologizing for the way I don't feel, justifying
my lack of interest to those who felt it was
warranted; so I guess it's kind of like that,
in a way.

I fell in love with someone once, a carcinogen
of a human being. I know what it's like
to come when you're called, to be controlled by
something. I know how it feels to confuse desire
with decay.

I saw a bird carrying a butt in its beak like it was
a savior, the other day.

I promised myself that would never be me.

WAYS YOU HAVE SAVED MY CONTACT INFO

Girl from the bar, wears red lipstick like a
stop sign, like an ambulance, like a
war cry, like a wound that never healed
properly; girl who bites her nails
too much, who orders a Tom Collins like the
most adorable 75-year-old to stay out past
8pm; girl who pushes her glasses up when
she's nervous; girl who leaves the cap off the
toothpaste, who forgot her earrings on your nightstand
when she wasn't even drunk;
crazy; girl who reminds you of your
mother; trouble; slut who only sleeps with
you; girl who finally
had
enough,

you change my name
in your phone again, something you're sure
I'll answer to: *girl that*
took your sharpened tongue and rounded it,

girl that took your muddled heart and turned it
into a poem.

HUBBLE TELESCOPE SPOTS CELESTIAL "EYE,"
A GALAXY WITH AN INCREDIBLY ACTIVE CORE

and I feel naked, suddenly, exposed in ways that run like dirt and blood down the shower drain. I cover my bellybutton with shaking hands. Energy bubbles up through my mouth, flows out through my fingers, seeps from my eye sockets; there is no containing it, and for the first time I am endless. I try to remember what made me hate the sight of my body if not its reflection in your irises. How they hold whole galaxies, flecks of dust and light and colors that haven't been named yet. How they grow dead when you look at me, like being seen by God and realizing your own grand
insignificance, the insipid
majesty
of your feeble existence.

I take photographs of you, for science—
so they can study it later, when there is nothing left,
and know that my universe wasn't always so empty,

but I end up burning every one of them.

HEARTBREAK SURVIVAL GUIDE

Monkey bars / and your mother's arms / and window shopping /
put on a black dress / take the back of your hand / press it to
potential new lovers' chests / see if that's where the fire is / use
up space / your bed is freezing / make a snow angel / rub your
hands together rapidly / get an empty vase and hold the lip to
your cheek, about midway / cry / cry more / keep crying / buy
yourself a bouquet / have it delivered / write a card to your new
body / cut the stems / arrange the flowers in the vase / use your
pain to keep something alive for a change / the only difference
between an anniversary and a funeral /

is the heartbreak

HERE WE GO 'ROUND THE MULBERRY BUSH

I try to write about broken hearts and it comes out
          merry-go-rounds / it comes out / bluebeard's ghost
          / it comes out / there was a violet streak to the way
          I loved you that I'm just now realizing was a bruise
I try to write about the old days and it comes out
          flower crowns / it comes out / birthday cakes / it comes
          out / I am not really much different now than the
          person I used to be / it comes out / water rings
I try to write about the look on your face and it comes out
          dead-end streets / it comes out / cityscapes / it comes
          out / try me / it comes out / coat buttons and /
          reindeer games and / windshield writing

These days I can't write anything without it sounding
          like an apology.

NEUTRON STAR

*Massive stars experience a most energetic and violent end, in which their remains are scattered about the cosmos in an enormous explosion called a supernova. Once the dust clears, the only thing remaining is a very dense star corpse known as a **neutron star**.*

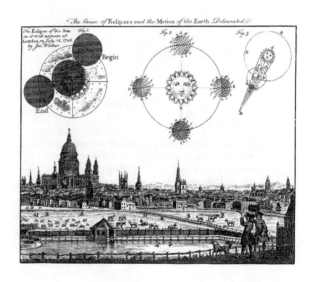

The Cause of Eclipses and the Motion of the Earth Delineated

THE CORNER OF FELICITY

This city
doesn't do earth
sounds, it speaks
in tongues,

otherworldly garbled
nonsense, she says
melted sugar,
she says
orange glaze,
don't listen, there is no
such thing
as listening, open
your mouth, concentrate on the
vibrations,
my bloodstream feels
buoyant, and willing;
this city says she
was here
before the Ice Age and the
Big Bang. The liquor
store around the corner
sells butterscotch pudding
that'll knock you dead,
and you'll say thank you
but it will sound
like cinnamon, and
yearning.

I was 26
when I moved here,
a little too young
for my age, I slept
alone
except for when
I didn't, I learned
to play the violin
on his heartstrings,
I learned there's no
such thing

as good whiskey, but
you don't drink it
for the taste.

This city
doesn't do earth sounds,
doesn't do love songs,
doesn't do good morning
texts, I tell you—just
a drum beat you hear as
a confession, a sax solo
that needs an RSVP, it's
okay
to be a little less, to be
a little more
than human when you
need to be, just some good
old-fashioned
soul trash, space garbage,
some crushed velvet in
your veins, just
goosebumps and
smoke rings, and you'd look
like a lava lamp if they
opened you up, honey.

You only hear it
if you forget everything you
know about everything, about
language, and logic, there's no
room here for biology, she says
lemon zest, she says
turmeric, she says
nape of my neck.

You lick your lips.

SELF-PORTRAIT AS A PEACH PIT

All the boys come away with
teeth chipped.

Hard, uneven thing. Folds,
like a fingerprint you cannot
trace, bone-bent shell kissed by
fleshy pink.
The skin tears. The veil breaks.
You hold it, thumb and forefinger,
a new home, a fresh casing,
the only part you cannot
digest properly, the only
morsel you don't have
permission
to taste.

The tangerine splits. The berry bleeds.
The peach lets you devour it
until

it doesn't.

Cyanide, and seed,
hard, uneven thing; a
flower blooming.

A stone at the center
of her being.

WHEN THEY ASK ME WHY I'M LIKE THIS

I say I / am drenched in soda water / and sweat / and subtle
manipulation / doused in quiet power / a closet hot-head /
a water sign setting herself on fire / sparks flying / caught
red-handed / dripping salt / and sex / and social standing
/ fixed / blood-soaked / wet / a waiting game. / I say we /
Scorpio girls / don't take your shit; / it's not a skill that we
inherited / and it doesn't come / easy. / I say I / am blessed /
with intuition / with original sin / with a lion's teeth / and a
woman's frame / and the good sense to use them both / as if
I was starving.

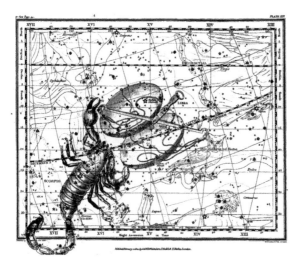

44

POSSIBLE SIGNS OF LIFE ON VENUS

i listened to John Mayer's *In Your Atmosphere* yesterday for the
first time since college. i used to fall asleep in my dorm room
to his live album, pretending not to realize the irony
of him performing a concert in a town to which he was singing
about never returning; pretending that wasn't a metaphor for
loving you and not loving you
simultaneously.

i know that if there exists a breathable gas around Venus, it can
only sustain life in theory. just like you had all the makings of a
soulmate on paper, but in the end it just wasn't practical. That
sometimes practice doesn't make perfect, it only makes you tired
and disappointed in ways you can't fully wrap your head around.
earth is more habitable than it has any right to be, but it's still
possible to burn upon entering, to explode upon impact.

death still happens here. we still stop
breathing.

      i bet you still tell her that you love her
      to the moon and back.

          tell me, where does that leave me?

I RUMMAGE THROUGH MY PAST LIVES
AND I FIND

a chariot, a noose,
a class ring that belonged to my mother, with a crack
in the centerpiece, Murphy's oil soap, and muddied truths,
and a wash basin; and every part of my body
a plane crash, a cut that never bleeds, a wound not made
for healing, a conspiracy; the shoes he used to wear before
that Christmas I bought him new, a box under the bed, and
I start to understand the things that scare us when we're
children, waves of nausea for no reason,
a wet cough,
a bobble-head,
a rosary that hasn't been held, a god that hasn't been
prayed to,

yet;

I pull out shards of broken glass and
old speeding tickets and the
business cards I used to mark my places
in books I never finished,

the amber spots in your irises,
red hair come loose,
the way the day breaks,

the number to reach you.

I have a habit of holding onto
things I know I'll never use.

LOVE AND ROCKETS: WE NEED TO FIGURE OUT
HOW TO HAVE SEX IN SPACE FOR HUMAN
SURVIVAL AND WELL BEING

But I say

we need to figure out how to have sex
on the ground—let's not get ahead of ourselves.
I am an animal, if nothing else, but I have recently been
at odds with intimacy in such a way that I no longer see myself
as a sexual being. Sex, lately anyway, feels more like a tragedy
I can't look away from, like a burn-out when it should be
a blast-off, cheers and wolf whistles, a success worth celebrating.
Let me be clear, when I talk about "well-being"—this is not about
the sex we are not having.
This is about how the sex we *are* having has riddled me with anxiety.
Radio static. Alarms going off. Systems malfunctioning.
Come (in), come (in).
Are you there?

Over.

My body has always been an excellent communicator, but
it's as if yours speaks
              another language.

WHO KNOWS HOW TO MAKE LOVE STAY?
another homage to Tom Robbins's <u>Still Life with Woodpecker</u>

1. Burn your initials in the tree out back. Toast with cheap
Seagram's and cranberry juice cocktail and complain about
the sugar. Love will tell you you're sweet enough already;
tell love it's full of shit. Laugh in each other's mouths, stretch
out, dirty the picnic blanket. When love asks you a question
about the universe, answer youngly, answer honestly, answer
with the depths of your naivety. Love will stay.

2. Tell love to pick a card. Fan them out between your fingers,
dancing over your chin and nose. The deck is a curtain and you
are the man behind it. Tell love to pay no attention. When love
starts to point or reach, tell love *not that one. Over a little. Keep
going.* When love picks the ace of hearts, tell love it must be
used to collecting such things. It will stay.

3. Gas the car up. Show up outside love's apartment at 3
in the morning. Don't honk the horn. Get out. Throw pebbles at
love's window. When that doesn't work, climb onto the second
story awning, tap lightly. When love presses its head to the glass,
tell it you need a copilot. Go on a road trip you haven't planned yet.
Let love navigate. Love will come home with you when you're
              ready.

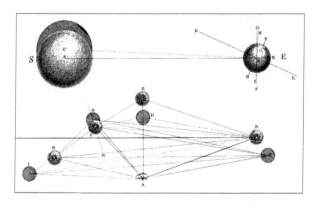

SOMETHING LIKE FIREWORKS

It's almost Jell-O shots and messy toasts o'clock,
spilling harsh liquid all over
my purse strings, all into my stomach;
it's almost dance music and
dresses meant for
warmer weather, it's almost empty
promises and empty drinks,
unmet goals and unmet
soulmates;
it's almost time to be
the same people
we used to be.

It's almost time ~~for the ball to drop~~ to drop the ball.
But if I can,
I will peel back my skin,
and remind myself I'm alive;
I will kiss my own lips,
hold my muscles bare,
tendons and all,
cut my limbs away from
the splintered stump of my body,
and you can cut me out of your
head if you want, out of your
pictures, with the sharp knife of her
sighs across your pillowcase.

By the morning,
I will have grown back,
one way
or another—
a stubborn tumor, a sickness that is
as much a part of you

as New Year's Day is a part of
New Year's Eve.

HOW NEUTRON STAR COLLISIONS FLOODED EARTH
WITH GOLD AND OTHER PRECIOUS METALS

Everything we know is just the result of
a bunch of different things smashing together.

I slammed my body into yours trying to make magic
and came away with apathy, came away with salt
in my wounds, came away with
nothing precious
to speak of.

My cavernous womb, black hole of
forbidden fruit, I stockpile apples
from the throats of men who
try to excavate me; collect bones from
boys who shine their light in my
dark places, try to discover things yet
unseen, my novelty naval, my obelisk
ovaries; try to name parts after themselves
that never belonged to them, try to lay claim,
plant flags, draft treaties using my blood as the ink.

Where they start settlements, I give them
earthquakes, I give them famine. Where they
build fences, I form hatchets of stomach
acid. Where they grow gardens, I bring only
drought, my desert tongue, a land untenable.

They stab their shovels into softened aorta, but
there is no gold here. Nothing precious
to speak of.

Where there is no oxygen inside me, I smother them
before they can regret having come
in the first place.

THINGS I AM SCREAMING TO THE UNIVERSE

I come calling for you because every time I go screaming
to God / he says, "go ask your Mother" / I did something messy /
how is it I stand here with a full grown woman's hips / with
a full grown woman's thighs / and yet at my core I still feel a
fifteen-year-old sickness in my stomach / do I entertain you /
do you scoff from on high / when I admit my faults, do you
root for me / do you know what it's like / to have been loved
so carelessly once that you spend the rest of your life worrying /
haunted by the ghosts of other people's pasts / losing a contest
you wrote the rules to / have you seen inside my head / have you
known the heartache of being a common convenience / a
happenstance / a makeshift soulmate / do you tell God not to be
so hard / on me / when I get like this / do you make him sleep on
the couch when you're angry / do you think I'm too dramatic /
was he right to call me / crazy / does being in the right place at
the wrong time / count for anything / call me / warm body / call
me / black hole / call me / band-aid / call me / by / any name /
but mine

51

SUBURBAN LEGEND

He said
he saw Bigfoot once,
and he waved, or she, or
they—he forgot to ask, but
anyway—Bigfoot waved, and
then went on making footprints
on the forest floor, and he said
he or she or they
smelled like the wanton
wishes of every stinking
mortal who walks upright and
has opposable thumbs
and thinks being
hairless of body makes
them
anything other than
naked.

He said
he saw a UFO once,
that it wasn't a plane
or a weather balloon,
or a reflection in his wire-
framed glasses—and you
can't tell him
otherwise—
he said there were no stars
that evening, but it went away
as quickly as it came, like
love, like lightning, as
fast as the morning,
that a vapor trail of
hope
and possibility was all
that remained, he said he saw
his mother's face
in the fading.

He left
before I could tell him

I am no
anomaly, no world
wonder, no mystery,

I am
the place where
things happen, I am
the setting,
I am the North
American wilderness,
the
night sky,
the expanse of the
universe, endless, the lack of
oxygen, the silence so
deep and vast
and wide it's the closest we'll
ever get to the absolute,
ultimate, big, bad,
unknowable

Nothing.

I am Loch Ness, if anything.

There's a monster
inside me
swimming around
that some people
claim

to have seen.

"WHAT DO WOMEN WANT?"
after Kim Addonizio

I want a telescope in the backyard,
you and me, on a blanket all dirt
and grass-stained, finding worlds too far
away to drive to.
I want a star named after me.
I want to unhinge my jaw, to swallow whole
Saturn's rings, and Pluto's moons, and
all the words I ever said
but didn't mean. I want them to taste like
green tea and apple cider vinegar and
youth and folly.
I want you to turn to me, like tide to shore,
and say the freckles on my shoulders
are more beautiful than the night sky. I want to roll my
eyes. I want to remember us, two kids in my
living room, listening to street fights on
the corner; how our backyard is quiet.
I want to make a galaxy of our lives; I want
everything else to burn up in our atmosphere;
I want the neighbors
to hear. I want to be the loudest, brightest thing
                    for miles and miles.

55

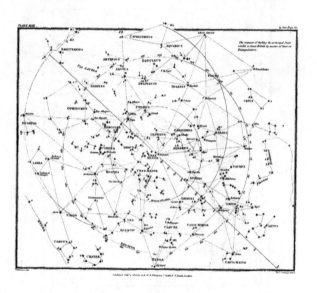

56

DID I EVER TELL YOU THAT YOUR MOUTH IS LIKE

fireflies, freshly bloomed cotton waving in the wind,
around 60 degrees, a hand on my belly, that is to say,
your mouth is like a sign of life, a conception, a well full
of blue ink. Like a matchstick between my teeth to stop my
eyes watering. Like the silken head of a baby bird under
my first two fingers. Like when I warm my hands in your
shirtsleeves. Like a flowing sieve.

I press myself against your lips, cold, like steel wrapped
in suede, that is to say, my body is like a shotgun with your
mouth around it, something you stare down the barrel of daily,
and your lips, a soft pillow, your tongue a muzzle, you search
for the trigger with your hips, and your mouth, your
delicate mouth, all gauze and cold compress,
and petroleum jelly,

a motive that can't break through
my teeth.

ON MAKING MYSELF BREAKFAST

When I say / I disassociate / what I mean is
I've been writing.
I have thought about
texting you, but I need to save
all I have to say.
I have taken two naps
since waking up this morning.

When I say / I'm okay / what I mean is

don't worry.
I checked the mail today. I did some
laundry. I was kissed goodbye and good
morning
simultaneously.

My biggest worry is whether I put too much
cinnamon
in the pancakes.

WORD PLAY

Do not tell me you love me
and call that poetry.
I have never had the words
for the grooves of your
fingerprints, how I could feel
each one of them on my stomach, for
the way your eyes unveiled flakes of
brownish-green in certain sunlight,
cattails jutting out, ponds for irises.

But do not tell me I'm pretty
and call that poetry.
Gasp
and fall back when I emerge
from the bedroom in my best
dress, introduce your mouth to my
neck when I'm just out of the shower
in the morning.
Make me late,
an inconvenience,
a nuisance,
a distraction.

I will lay my clothes across your floor
and call that poetry.

I'm so tired of all this
talking.

WHETSTONE

Sometimes I read old messages we exchanged, and I throw
up in my mouth a little.

Sometimes I still get a knot in my stomach.

If these emails she sent about the two of you getting back
together were a person, they'd be old enough to ride a bike
without training wheels. My hostility would be getting
her period, and shoplifting earrings from Claire's, and
joining the soccer team.

As a grown-up, I try to think of you as a lesson learned too
early, proof I was never the gifted student I believed myself
to be—who could ace the test without even
studying.

I try to think of you as a thing I did poorly, and I
hate doing things poorly, so I think that's why
it still nags at me.

(All that aside—)
Thank you for being a pretty stone
where I could grind my teeth.

It's been a long time, but they've come in quite nicely.

MASS EFFECT

And now that I have traveled at
warp speed across the galaxy
to save these people from
themselves, to unite all races and
creeds and
species against
a common enemy, I wonder
if everything
is really as simple
as perspective.

If given the option, I would sacrifice myself
every time, but that doesn't make me a
leader.

Destroy or *Control*—
I mean what does that say
about intelligent life, that those
are the choices we are left with
in the end?

It's amazing
how often the villain
in the story isn't really
the villain. Or at least,

it makes me uncomfortable
to admit
how often

I agree with them.

OBIT

after Victoria Chang

Wonder—died August 21, 2017, wearing a black T-shirt
with white print, watching a solar eclipse from behind cheap,
plastic shades. Proceeded in death by Enthusiasm, Optimism,
and the Belief in Fate and Magic and Soulmates. It was survived
by my aunt's backyard, overrun with honeysuckle and sycamore
trees, the smell was almost sweet enough to taste. It was night at
2:30pm, a brief moment when I wasn't in awe of my ability to be
lonely while surrounded by people who love me. How a
once-in-a-lifetime occurrence became just another something
I'd lived through. An anomaly turned mediocre, like going back
to you every time, in spite of everything. The day I realized you
and this wonderous thing had too much in common for comfort,
that I didn't owe you my astonishment.
Showing up unannounced in the middle of the day.
Shrouding my world in darkness. Leaving as suddenly.

When everything was said and done, my grandmother took her eyes
off the sky, looked around at us and said, "That's all it is?"

It had the disenchanted ring of a eulogy to it.

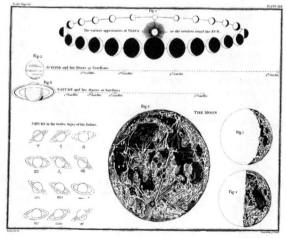

62

AFTER A 3.5 MILLION-YEAR HIATUS, THE LARGEST
COMET EVER DISCOVERED IS HEADED OUR WAY

They announce our demise
like it's a 90's boy band reunion tour.

It's been a long time since we saw them,
but all those frozen gases are ready to rock your face off.
For one night only, they'll be back in action,
replaying all their old hits.
Get ready for a night you'll never remember.

Coming to a city near you. Tickets on sale now.

Largest Comet Ever Discovered, featuring
Total Devastation and
Maximum Casualties,
with a special guest appearance by
*Is the End of Life as We Know It Enough to Make Us Love Each Other
Again?*

FOCUS ON (ANYTHING BUT) YOUR BREATHING

I count your freckles like kitchen
tiles.
Every breath labored, a day at the
lake. In through the nose, out through the
mouth. I can taste the sulfur, the smoke
in my face. I am
covered in charcoal
and chicory.

I sing the only song I know the
words to, it's all you have heard for
weeks, but you haven't complained.
We warm our hands on
anything,
        your cigarette,
                burning
        my coffee,
                burning
        the world
                as we know it.
                (burning).

The scraps of paper in my stomach, creases
of poems on pages half-written,
act as kindling. The embers hold council
inside me. Up 'til now, I've been so careful,
but I long for the way your pillow
clings to your shampoo, the way it
conjures dreams
worth falling asleep to, worth
never waking.

In through the nose. Out.

SOME NIGHTS YOU DANCE WITH TEARS IN YOUR EYES

and i mistake them / for stars / for diamonds / for sparkling
wine / i have felt the pull of your arms like the earth's gravity
/ like the moon pulls the tide / i have been the ocean for you / i
have gone out and come back / too many times / but it is always
the same motion / unchanging / and i'm sorry / there is music
bouncing off the walls of my chest cavity / and you hear it /
muffled / a song enveloped in cotton / a just-opened pill bottle /
you grab for me when you need to feel / more okay / i make the
bad things go away / for a while / i make my hand a
handkerchief / i wipe away the night like sleep from your eyes /
the waning sunrise / the balmy morning / the mouthy
afternoon / i become to sun / to save you / i dry your skin /
without even /

touching you.

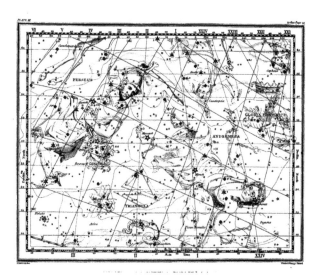

MY MOTHER TELLS ME WE WOULD
MAKE BEAUTIFUL BABIES

and the hollow tin chest that is my womb grows smaller.

my biological clock will soon chime 30,
my hourglass figure will
soon run out, and I do not have room in here
to carry a child with all this guilt.

every time someone asks,
I can almost feel it kicking.
my deepest fear is that one day
you will start asking, too.

TURN THE LIGHT OFF BEFORE YOU GO

The second time you fall in love, it should
be with a city;

a place for which your heart feels homesick,
where your soul is a refugee, everywhere else
is war-torn, and you're fleeing.

Growing up somewhere doesn't mean
it's where you'll do your most
growing.

When I go back home now,
I seem out of context. I never really
call it "home"
anymore without   hesitating,
without feeling it like a sweater shrunk
in the wash, the words don't fit inside
my mouth anymore, they don't
cover me.

"Home" is not
a force of habit; home is something
else entirely.

Leaving
was the hardest, most beautiful
thing I ever did; (it doesn't make me
like him.

          It doesn't make me
                    like him.)
I'd do it again.

SWEET RED

I have become / a reflection of Christmas tree lights /
and a half foot of snow / fresh / and cold / a compilation
of peach moonshine / and cheap Roscato / I am more my
mother's daughter / than ever in these moments / warm
cheeks / red nose / I can't tell / who I belong to more / in these
moments / you / or me / (it's probably you) / all I know is /
the faint glow of yellow against hardwood floor / against
eggshell walls / gives me the smallest hope / a gift I didn't
ask for / the feeling that my life isn't just an endless loop of /
working / and sleeping / and watching TV / and I don't mind
those / but occasionally I need / to forget everything / to spend
the evening / loving you / and out of my mind a little / and still
loving you when I don't have my faculties / and I will / and I
will / and I will hold you like the road holds the cold / like the
room holds the air until you enter it / like the reason for the
season / is a myth / like there doesn't always have to be a reason

to be happy /

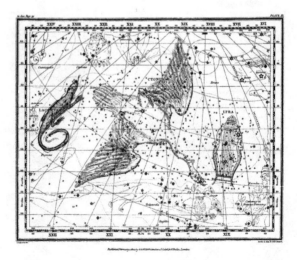

ON THE AIR IN YOUR LUNGS

// The inside
of the human body
sounds like outer space.
I am a meteor shower,
a supernova, a solar
flare—something too
bright
and far away
to be touched, but still
you reach.

Anything can go wrong.
Anything.

But how breathtaking. //

MEMOIR OF A TWENTY-SOMETHING

I started crying at TV commercials. I noticed my mother's
hands feel like soft suede; I wear her eyes like
hand-me-down diamonds, her voice pours out of my mouth
some mornings like smooth cream into donut shop coffee.

I saw the end of a first love. I saw the last of a new love. I
left loose hair all over jersey sheets and bathroom sinks; I
covered my front seat with tarnished rings and mixed cd's,
and a flattened quarter dangling from my rearview.

I wrote you a poem and called it a postcard and called it
the truth and called it a eulogy.
I wrote you a letter and it wasn't an apology.

My muscles stopped rubbing my bones the wrong way;
my joints started popping like fireworks on the lake,
so I made myself a holiday. A bottle of champagne.
Heavy arms and gritty teeth.

I left and I left and I left and I
stayed.

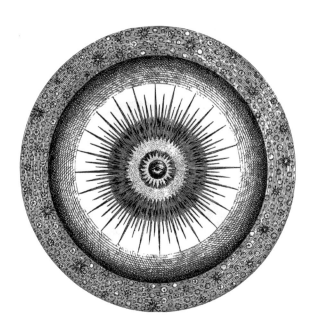

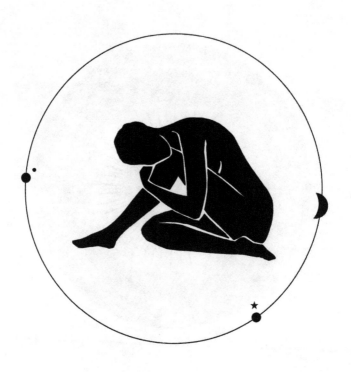

BLACK HOLE

*If an especially massive star explodes, it can form a **black hole** which absorbs all light that touches it. In this stage, objects are attracted towards the star due to a tremendous increase in gravitational force.*

WHEN I SAY I STILL LOVE YOU I MEAN

barely.
I mean
there is a train to where you are on any given
day, and I never take it.
I mean I always look at the clock when it's displaying
your birthday, and a little part of me
celebrates.

I got used to your laughter reverberating in my
chest, your hands shaking as you light your
cigarette, your eyelashes gyrating like a line dance
when you sleep, your chattering teeth, and

when I say I still love you, with my bed half-empty, and
my breath gone shallow, I just mean
it isn't stirring—
it is still

      it is still

           it is still.

THE OLDEST GAMMA-RAY BURST EVER
DISCOVERED WAS JUST A PIECE OF SPACE JUNK

Some people talk about firsts like they are something
worth romanticizing, and I'll admit that I used to be one
of them. Like love isn't something you need to work the
kinks out of, like soulmates can't be variables, like they
aren't interested in
results
at all.

Now I laugh
at the way you hypothesized that no one else
would ever love me.

If the oldest gamma-ray burst ever discovered was just a
piece of space junk, then can you imagine the unholy
pedestal I've held you up on—while our love was not an
anomaly, was not a world wonder, was not a miracle of
science or religion either one?

I made my body an experiment; I tested your hypothesis.

I discovered a love no one else had ever known, and
lo and behold, they named it after me.

ALTERNATIVES TO APOLOGIZING

There are a number of studies on how women
apologize too much, and I assume they have
something
to do with you.

So I start carrying daisies with me, and giving
them to people I bump into on the street, I start
writing poems instead of thank-you notes, I send
them to my exes, to my almost-exes, to friends I've
lost touch with, I send one to your mom for how
warmly she welcomed me, I send her a piece of
twine for every reason it didn't work out between
us. She crafts them into a holiday wreath.

I catch the word "sorry" in the net of
my throat; I turn my tongue into a dictionary.

See also: selfish; exhausted; beautiful; free.

AND ALL ALONG, THE PERSON I MOST NEEDED
TO FORGIVE WAS ME

Whatever
you had to do
to get where you are now,
it's okay. You know
in your bones
it was a necessary

evil.

All the things you have done
in order to claw your way out
and remain somewhat
intact, the manipulation, and toxicity,
and the leaving—these were just
makeshift buoys you built to survive
a turbulent sea—they do not make you
the same as the men who only
taught you density.

Forgiveness
is a light in the pit of your stomach,
a fire on the hearth of your lungs
that must be stoked.
You collected enough driftwood
to turn yourself into
a home.

It's okay to be warm there.

SCIENTISTS FINALLY HAVE AN EXPLANATION FOR THE
MOST ENERGETIC EXPLOSIONS IN THE UNIVERSE

My body stopped popping
and cracking the day
that I met you; as if my bones
were saying, *yes, right here—*

this is exactly where
we should be.

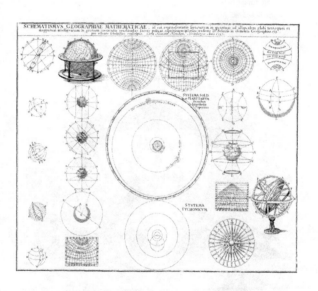

AN ODE TO THE BORING
after Amy Kay

Build a shrine to the relief-sounds we make
getting into bed each evening,

the branch on this timeline we get to occupy together—
just past wanton youth but not quite middle
age.

I forget to lay the chicken out, so we order
restaurant food to-go, again, and eat it on the couch.

Cherish the ill-advised back cracks on the hardwood,
the butt pinches for tax, the dog breath disagreements.

You run out to get milk at 10:30pm so I can have
chocolate cake tonight and iced coffee in the morning,
and I insist it's too much trouble, but I'll admit
the performance is not my most convincing.

Sometimes, I think, what are the odds that I would find
someone I want to spend every stupid,
insignificant day with? I add up all the times
you've fallen asleep—phone in hand—
scrolling through Reddit; I multiply it
by the number of post-it notes you've written me,
and I realize
that is math
            I cannot even do.

INSTRUCTIONS FOR NAMING CATERPILLARS

plant some milkweed in the backyard and hope the neighbor kids
don't get into it. check the planter every morning. count how
many caterpillars you see. check thoroughly, on your hands and
knees. like an earth-toned Where's Waldo. (three). count them the
next day. (three). check if it's supposed to rain. if it isn't,
improvise. if you don't have nature-made, tap water will do just
fine. press a finger down into the soil to make sure it's wet
enough. if the dirt sticks loosely to your knuckle, it's perfect. if
your finger comes away slick and mostly clean, you've gone too
far. basically, the opposite of checking if brownies are ready.

now wait. be patient. count them the next day. (four). and the
next day. (seven). again. (nine). now what should we call them?
don't think about it too much. the first name that comes to mind.
(Carl). your uncle's name. (Bill). okay, okay, now take a deep
breath. there's no rush,
right?

it's a metamorphosis, isn't it?

becoming takes time.

MY LOVE LANGUAGE MUST BE:
after Zane Frederick

whatever comes off your tongue, honestly / a lullaby
all covered in salt / and whiskey / sleeping in every morning /
a plastic cup full of vodka / and white cran-peach / all grace /
and patience and / mercy / mercy / mercy /

when the dog grunts at us because his water bowl is empty /
and you get up without me even asking / and you talk to him /
the whole time / as he does those tippy-taps with his feet /
against the kitchen laminate / and you're both so / excited /

when i'm singing / in the car / to music i loved when i was /
sixteen / and even then it was / about you / without me
knowing / and i chose it / on purpose / for this road trip,
specifically / but that's beside the point / and anyway, i'm
singing / and you say / "what song is this?" / and i can't help /
but know / you were listening /

THE VIEW OF US FROM SPACE

I paint myself in past mistakes and call it painting
the town red, call it shedding my skin, call it

bleeding; you take up a collection for the broken parts
of my body, fashion my bones into a jungle gym, something
meant for play, you weave in and out of my ribcage until

my heart is no longer covered in weeds. There's a fine line
between love and hate but that's like saying the earth
is just a blip in the universe; it is,
but it doesn't feel that way when you're

in it. I have had a love like being pushed down on the
playground, I have had a love like pigtail pulling; I have been
loved to death, to the moon and back; that is to say,
I have been
loved
without oxygen.

Yours is the only love that feels
                              like breathing.

JESUIT

I cannot help but feel like
the only girl you've ever
loved while wearing that
high school sweatshirt.

I know I am wrong, but
sometimes,

I feel so young.

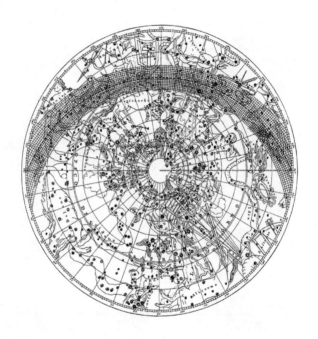

HOW TO SAVE US (LOVE IN THE TIME OF COVID-19)

- a bistro set as front porch furniture
- my hand on the back of your neck
- I like lying in bed with you late, because our bed is a place
  where we're the only two welcome
- they closed all the bars in the city so we drink at home now
- you kiss every part of my face indiscriminately and
- I giggle, almost 30 years old and yet I giggle, and so
- you keep kissing me
- every time you come home you wash your hands
- you wipe down our phones
- I ask you how your day was
- in the infinite process of my waking, you tell me
  good morning each time my eyes open
- it is

KITCHEN CONVERSATIONS

i tell you / the milk has gone sour / again /
and the pineapple has gone bad / still sitting /
on the counter / never bothered to cut it open /
we do that enough / to ourselves / as it is /
i tell you / you're hovering / that i need space
while i place the turkey on the bread / but the
truth is / you are the only person for whom
"too close" doesn't exist /

i tell you / the dishes are dirty / i tell you / we're
out of paper towels / i tell you / dinner will be ready
in five minutes / and you say / just enough time
for a dance / you tune your smart phone to the /
Bluetooth speaker on the windowsill above the sink /
and you say / this kitchen is not a cookhouse / this
kitchen is not a scullery / this kitchen is a ballroom /
this kitchen is a two-person rave / i stand there / and i
take your hand / and we laugh / and sway / and i always
leave more full / and less hungry

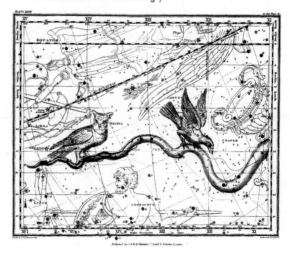

LIBIDO SNAP

*(n.) The quick, vague flicker of arousal that you don't
share with your partner, because you don't really feel like
having to get naked and have sex.*

You lick batter off the mixing
spoon, and I think about
how cold the room is, how many layers
we're wearing. It seems I always
want to have sex with you
when we're in the middle of something,
when we have to finish cooking, when
the movie is really getting good.
And suddenly I am a mathematician
with a sweet tooth. How long will it probably
take, if you add the initial kissing; will the
undressing be good-things-come-to-those-who-wait or
just-move-everything-to-the-side-already; will there
be foreplay; 1/3 c. oil, 1/4 c. water, 2 eggs
that I cracked single-handed;
you said it was
sexy.

I laugh at the chocolate on your chin,
the early stages of a brownie not viable yet,
and I hand you a napkin.

I set a timer for twenty minutes.

SPECIAL PROBLEMS IN VOCABULARY
after Tony Hoagland

For lack of a better word, I tell you I
love
you, but what I really mean is
there is a sunset in your eyes that I want to
catch every night until time ends.

Crow's feet stretch from your eyelids like the last dying
rays, cling with rose-red fingers to the way you look at me
when you come home and I'm half-awake.

I find your eyelash on my cheek and lose the concept
of wish-making.

All the times you say something
so weird, and so random, that the well of
gratitude inside me bubbles into a geyser,
bursts through the hole in my face in the most
succinct way I can manage—

what I really mean is
you give me the sensation of drowning
in a good way, of overflowing without having
a mess to clean up afterward,
but they haven't
invented a word for that yet,

have they?

WAYS I DESCRIBE YOU TO FRIENDS
YOU HAVEN'T MET YET

/ you are the only one who sees all the beautiful things I do
that I don't post on the internet /
/ you are my favorite Friday night plans /
and Saturday morning / and Sunday afternoon /
/ your parents have a happy marriage, and it shows /
/ you prefer your rooms dim and your food cold /
/ you are so, so good that the bad just rolls off your back like
small nothings /
/ you have a bigger part of me than anyone else has, and
that scares me and at the same time that doesn't scare me /
/ i've tried to turn so many boys into poetry; you were poetry
already /

IF DEATH IS A CRASH COURSE

it taught me (how to) cook for one.
how to lose composure at the sound of trumpets.
how to pray, but not how to (believe).
it taught me regret and shame and how to
carry them neatly, folded up (in) the back pocket
of my jeans. it taught me bereavement lasts longer
than three days, but (the world) keeps moving. it
taught me to hate cemeteries, and hometowns,
and holidays. it taught me life is composed of
parentheses.

you always said there is no remedy (like) a shot of
Tennessee whiskey and an hour of afternoon sleep.

i keep (your) old radio on a shelf in my library, and it
occurs to me i have become adept at hoarding.

if loss is a skill, i have honed it until it's cut me.
if (grief is) an art, consider this (a masterpiece).

nobody,not even the rain,has such small hands
after E.E. Cummings

should I drift off to sleep, pay my dream-speech no
attention; I have not a poet's bone in my body, but your
eyelashes come to me like quill pens, l o n g, and belonging
to some beautiful animal, and
blacker than they have any
right to be.
The amphitheater
          of my mind
pushes me to the podium, I picture everyone naked,
but you are the only one in attendance; the spotlight
echoes off (your body and for
a moment,i am blind,and for a moment,i see

everything
there is. I hear

Nothing
but) the sound

of you clapping in the distance.

THE ANATOMY OF
A FLUTTER

When it comes
to loving you,
I am neither the caterpillar
nor the butterfly.

I am the chrysalis.

I will hold you until
there is nothing
but beauty.

WE KEEP GOING TO OTHER PEOPLE'S WEDDINGS

2 parts Pinot Grigio to 1 part Dua Lipa

This is where the magic happens.
I take my shoes off,
leave them
in the chair marked by your
suit coat—a metaphor for my
inhibitions. They are too uncomfortable
to dance in.

You twerk to lyrics about apple bottom jeans,
knowing full well you have no ass
to speak of. I know all the words
from muscle memory.

The crease of your suit, the way it fits you
drives me a little crazier than I'm used to.

We already know what our song is going to be.

But these occasional late nights, our same old routine,
our scrabble tile fights, getting drunk way too easily—

you are
the only soundtrack I need.

REASONS TO LOVE YOU

1. You get restless when you're on the phone
with your therapist, so you make the bed.

2. Your laugh comes out suddenly like the squawk of a
bird, matches mine like the echo of a yodel
in the mountains.

3. There are moments when I kiss you, and you taste
of a time much more innocent.

4. Your parents are still together, so you believe in love
in ways that I've lost faith in.

5. You do the dishes.

6. You do the laundry.

7. You dance like a ninety-year-old man with surprisingly
wide range of motion. Or a Sim.

8. You wake up smiling, and I will never understand it.

9. The gap between your teeth.

10. Your premature crow's feet.

11. How you've made me feel, after everything,
like it is safe to be happy.

      12. *Because.*

NOT WITH A WHIMPER BUT A SIGH OF RELIEF

My deepest fear is that the world
will end on a Wednesday,

that our clumsy hands will never find
another weekend, that the start of another
work week will be all that remains, that
our last breath will feel like waking up early.

I don't welcome that alarm tone in my
head for eternity.

It is Sunday morning, and my bed
becomes a beach towel, the sun streaming through
blinds, your lungs become a seashell, the sound of you
breathing, like ocean waves
next to me.

I want this to be
the last thing I remember,
the swell, the crash, the call of the sea—

the crest of loving each other at our own leisure.

BRIGHT SKIES

Your eyes are grey—I think—
almost three years later and I still haven't bothered
to learn what color
your eyes are. I admit, maybe, I don't think about it,
because historically I have been a girl who's only loved
blue-eyed boys, and maybe,
I don't like to confront my own rule breaking.

Your hair is oak tree root, dying acorn, medium
brown with an occasional glint of lightspeed white.
Your mouth is rose-breasted cockatoo, San Francisco
salt ponds pink, too deep to walk across, the Red Sea
to my Moses tongue, parting.
Your skin, the palms of your hands like sand dunes,
cracked, sunflower seed tan and some days honeybee
golden, arms open like holy gates to welcome me.

The color of 2022 will be "Bright Skies," according to
paint manufacturer Dulux.

But you
are the sun's light at every wavelength, the
sky in all weathers, in all conditions,
a timelapse of unbridled
existence—lavenders and ceruleans and
tangerines and magentas;
vermilion and amethyst, cobalt and chartreuse.

There is so much more
to the heavens

than blue.

THE THOMAS LETTERS
in the style of Lemony Snicket's The Beatrice Letters

Steadily. Through time and space.

With cautious abandon and unbridled ease. With the slow burn of haste.

I will love you as the squirrels love our bird feeder, as risk loves reward,
as the jewel-heavy crown of a spring day fits the frame of our back porch.
That is to say, well. I will love you until jazz notes stop bouncing off this
cobblestone city, until the swamp finally succumbs to the unwavering
concrete. I will love you with no concern for disdainful looks from downtown
passers-by, with no concept of kissing too much or laughing too loudly, as if
our ordinary lives are vacation enough. I will love you as the rain loves
the tin roof. That is to say, obnoxiously. I will love you as if we're sneaking
away together, and on occasions we do happen to sneak away, I will love you
as the summer loves ending, as the tide loves the shore, as every person
sitting at every table around us loves staring at their phone. That is to say,
I will love you without thinking. I will love you until my brain is too full, and
when there is no room in my head left to love you another second, I will slip
into a vegetative state. Quietly. Happily. Like a big toe into a hot tub. I will
love you as a coma loves company. Still. As soft as a machine hum, as delicately
as a ripple on the lake, a sink dripping, an EKG. That is to say, with eyelids heavy,
with muscles atrophied, with mouth closed and lips dried and bed sores forming,
as long as my heart beats, it will be saying, "I love you," in some cosmic way.
In forms of language that have been lost, or that haven't been invented yet,
in this life and the next, and in the lifetimes before we met.

Unequivocally. Inconceivably. I will love you like today loves the
possibility of tomorrow, like tomorrow loves the
never-ending certainty

of today.

SCIENTISTS DETECT RADIO SIGNALS FROM
GALAXY'S CENTER, HAVE NO CLUE WHAT IT IS

It's a wailing inside of my chest, a battle cry, a scarlet
bellow, that's all; it's a hurricane siren, a thunder crash,
hail on a tin roof in the town I grew up in; it's you singing
in the shower; it's me singing in the car, your mouth making
trumpet sounds, the first song we ever danced to in the kitchen,
the first time we said *I love you* and it came out like a church
bell, like a clock chime, like a train whistle; *thank god, it's time,*
you're here; it's a snore in the darkness, a snort in the daylight;
it's me calling out to whoever's responsible, through whatever
means you heard my voice in the void of the life I used to have,
and you followed it;

It's my steady heartbeat chanting

> *thank you,*
> *thank you,*
> *thank you.*

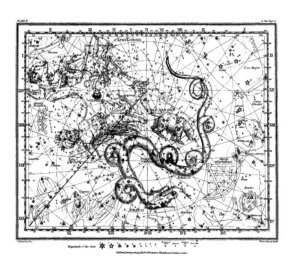

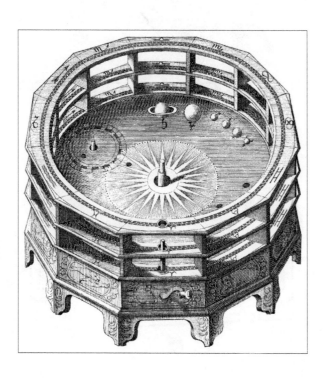

WHEN THE WORLD ENDS I WILL

1. hold your hand a little more tightly, at the
last minute, like a quiet prayer, like an expression
of gratitude, like a colossal fuck you to all the times I
thought I would leave this world lonely
2. open my arms into the blinding, infamous
void, let my eyelashes kiss each other with boundless
longing, embrace the unimaginable, insurmountable
nothing, believe it is everything in spite of its name,
be full as well as empty
3. think not for a second of the things I find unfair,
or infuriating, or bleak; of the horrors, or the pains,
or the plagues
4. be immersed only in the ways our fingerprints fit
together, like tiny gears, their echoing click, how my
existence only works when yours is there with it

HOW TO KEEP GOING

I cherish mornings when you sleep in with me because they are so rare. I always set my alarm for 7:30 but sleep until 8:45, because every time I roll over to press snooze, I pull you— as if with gravitational force—and you become an outline of my body, pressed behind me, my curves sync up with your grooves, a grandfather clock of the two of us, and it's so comforting that I decide the world can wait a while.

And I realize that's it. That's how to keep going.

Hold the thing that you love as tight as you can,
and when the world comes knocking,
hold up one finger;

tell it you'll be there
in a minute.

ON ETERNITY

This is not about waiting. This is about patience, or how I
stopped measuring my life in spans of time, stopped measuring
my waistline, my happiness in Sunday drives, stopped treating
each poem like a cemetery.

I lied to my body; I still lie to my body. There is no difference in
being here and being infinite, and too often I forget that this
moment is every second that's ever existed.

They say the process of star formation takes around a million
years from the time the initial gas cloud starts to collapse until
the star is created. The leftover material from the star's birth is
used to form planets and other celestial anomalies—like you.
And me.

But this is not about waiting.
This is about stargazing, how you connect the freckles on my
back into constellations with a felt tip Sharpie, or what
the color blue means.

If every atom in the universe is derived from the same stuff
just space gunk, just star fragments, just
cosmic dust, if life and death are just the universe recycling, then
we have spent billions of years as a single entity.
We have already been together forever.

We always will be.

IF THERE ARE INFINITE PARALLEL UNIVERSES

then somewhere, i am softer / less irritable / dance more /
i imagine it's like before we knew each other / living lives
side-by-side that have everything to do with the other / not
knowing it / right now, we are fucking on the counter / we are
painting bookshelves in the library / we are fighting about
money / about work / about nothing / maybe hauntings are
just different universes overlapping / meeting up at the worn
spots / i see you at the end of the hallway one morning and
mistake you for a ghost / it doesn't occur to me you are alive
somewhere else /

we are alive in so many places / why can't it be here?

ABOUT THE POET

Michelle Awad has only recently grown into calling herself
a poet. So much so, now, that she's branded herself with it.
Tennessee native turned New Orleanian, she firmly believes
in going where your heart no longer feels homesick.
She believes in staying there as long as you can.

More than anything, she has an inkling that space and time
are on our side. That aliens are real. That there are little
pieces of the celestial inside all of us. That sometimes, they
resemble each other. That sometimes, they connect.

In her spare time, you can find her sitting on her back porch
in Algiers with a telescope and that idiot she's in love with,
sipping a gin cocktail and listening to the sounds of the city.
Her dog is probably there, too, protecting the yard from
squirrels.

@THECONSTANTPOET